the new apartment

Edition 2005

Author: Arian Mostaedi
Publisher: Carles Broto
Editorial Coordinator: Jacobo Krauel, Joan Fontbernat
Graphic designer & production: Pilar Chueca
Text: contributed by the architects,
edited by Amber Ockrassa, William George and Marta Rojals

© Carles Broto i Comerma
Jonqueres, 10, 1-5
08003 Barcelona, Spain
Tel.: +34 93 301 21 99
 Fax: +34-93-301 00 21
E-mail: info@linksbooks.net
www. linksbooks.net

the new apartment

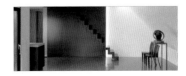

INTRODUCTION

The dwelling is the warm and pleasant refuge in which we feel protected, our place of rest and work, the scenario in which our daily life is enacted, the space in which the essence of each biography is best revealed, a place of encounter and confrontation in which we spend most of our time.

Interior design is currently one of the most innovative disciplines of architecture. Contemporary architects are aware that there is a need for multifunctional and polyvalent spaces and at the same time highly defined spaces that are pleasant and calm and make their inhabitants feel comfortable. They attempt to meet the needs of the 21st century through the interplay of interior and exterior and the integration with the surroundings. Two basic elements in their work are the combination of materials such as wood, glass and steel, and the bold use of open spaces with hardly any divisions, in which light becomes a basic element of the deign.

The search for bold and completely original forms that are adapted to the lifestyle of their inhabitants is often another factor that leads to experimentation and creativity with forms and materials.

This volume presents a wide range of proposals and styles that show the tendencies and ideas of a new interior architecture in which there seems to be no place for unnecessary decorative concessions, and the challenge focuses on creating a space as a sanctuary in which to take refuge from chaos.

Eldridge Smerin

Armitage Hall

Photographs: Lyndon Douglas

London, UK

The apartment is a former assembly hall within a substantial 1920s central London building. Eldridge Smerin has converted the space into a 4500-square-foot (418 sq m) apartment on three levels. The existing 19.7-foot-high (6 m) assembly room has been transformed into living space with a kitchen, bar and private film screening space beyond. The enormity of the main volume is animated at the upper level by a series of glass-fronted projecting elements which provide new internal elevations to the bedrooms behind them.

The bedroom elements are steel-framed structures clad in lacquer-finished panels. To avoid introducing any load on the floor below, each element is a separate structure hung from a deep steel beam concealed above the ceiling that spans between the front and rear elevations of the existing building.

Each incorporates its own adjacent bathroom; that serving the main bedroom includes a sunken bath and walk-in shower clad in marble, all hidden behind a mirrored wall. Against this new upper-level contemporary elevation, the full height windows of the building's facade have been retained in the main space, framing views of the city beyond.

In a light well to the rear, a new accommodation block clad in glazed brickwork has been constructed on columns off the base of the light well to form the film screening room and flood the entrance lobby from the elevator and stair with light.

The roof of this new block also forms a terrace off the main bedroom, screened by a wall of black-stemmed bamboo. The lower level of the apartment is finished throughout with a dark timber floor, which is equipped with underfloor heating. The kitchen and bar areas incorporate units finished in contrasting white or black high gloss lacquer. The lighting, audio and visual systems throughout are all centrally controlled.

Pod structure

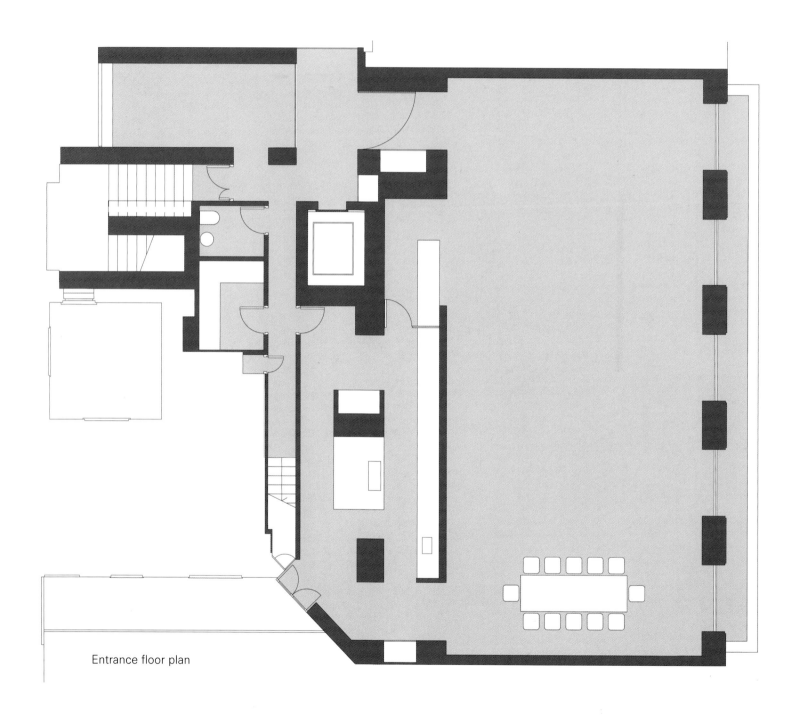

Entrance floor plan

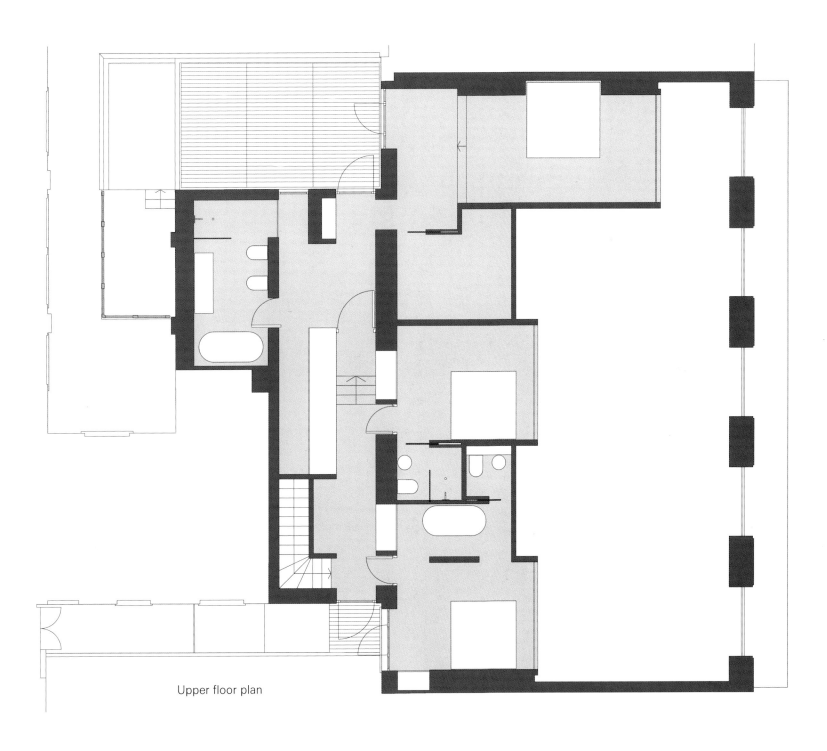

Upper floor plan

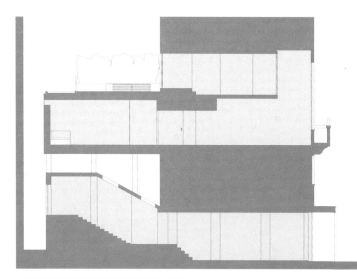

Cross section

The bathroom serving the main bedroom, which is concealed behind a mirrored wall, includes a sunken bath and walk-in shower clad in marble. The lower level is floored almost exclusively in dark timber and equipped with underfloor heating.

Combarel & Marrec

Fiat Loft

Photographs: Benoît Fougeirol

Paris, France

The site for the project is the back end of a Parisian block mainly occupied by workshops. The building sits on what used to be a light-filled backyard which was gradually filled in with built structures. Subsequently, the building itself is wedged in tightly among other buildings that are mostly higher than it. Bringing light into the house, therefore, became a central concern in the new design.

The volume to be restructured was composed of three different spaces: the covered backyard (a makeshift glass roof had been put in place at some point), the basement and a spare room located in the raised ground floor, which was not accessible from the building's stairwell.

The only way of ensuring a modicum of natural light in this hemmed in site was via a glass roof. The challenge and aim therefore became applying the same qualities and status of a conventional façade to a horizontal plane, which also had to bear certain necessary characteristics of ceiling and roof.

The roof and all its components are at the service of the views and natural light. The envelope has been conceived as a sort of periscope which goes in search of fragments of the sky and the surrounding built landscape, bringing them back down into the apartment for the enjoyment of its inhabitants.

The light and environment are thereby broken up and re-assembled into a composed image. The glass roof becomes an oversized kaleidoscope offering a shifting, fragmented image of the surroundings.

An exterior volume - the courtyard - has been set up in the interior of the layout and capped by the glass roof as an inversion of the sheltered surfaces.

The entire apartment is assembled around this inverted room, which is framed with floor-to-ceiling sliding glass panels that allow a complete reorganization of the interior space, depending on how much intimacy is desired.

The building occupies what used to be a light-filled courtyard which has been filled in with built structures over the years and, consequently, is hemmed in by taller buildings. Since a conventional façade was out of the question, the challenge was to treat a horizontal plane both as roof and façade.

Existant floor plan

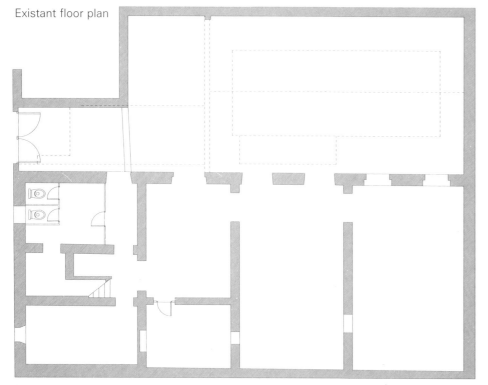

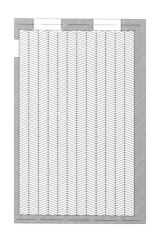

Ground floor plan

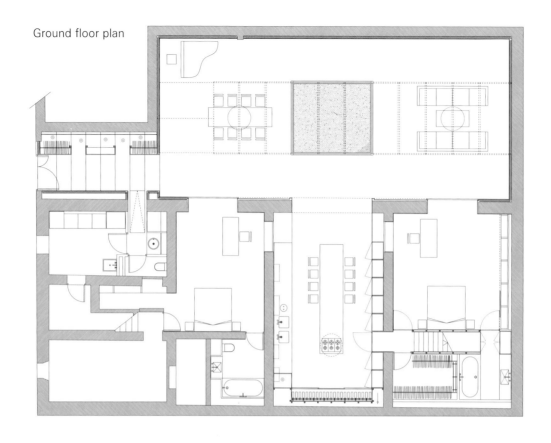

First floor plan

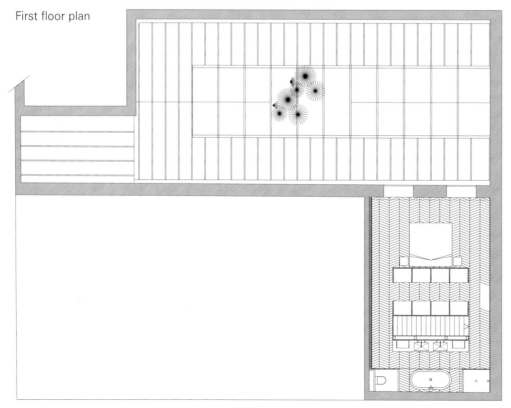

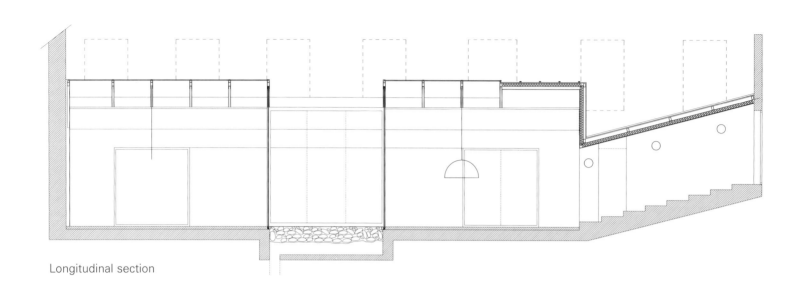

Longitudinal section

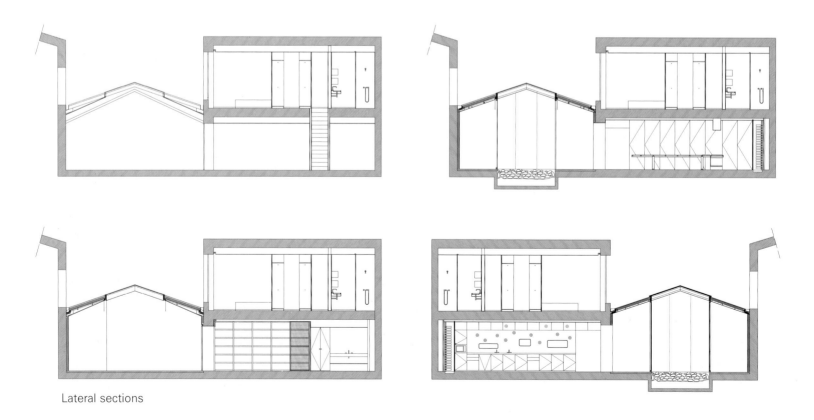

Lateral sections

Cho Slade Architecture

Van Doren Apartment

Photographs: Jordi Miralles

New York, USA

This two storey apartment on Fifth Avenue is designed to be a pied-a-terre for an art dealer. The apartment was organized into an open living/entertainment space on the first floor and a private bedroom/home office on the second floor.

In the entry, a sculpted, curved plaster wall unifies what were three separate wall panels into a single gesture and emphasizes the window opening in the entry space. Here, the floor is a white terrazzo.

The first floor powder room and kitchen are contained within a seamless Sapele-covered box. The kitchen itself is carved out of this box and is clad entirely in a pale green Corian. The monolithic surfaces accentuate the idea of a single solid mass: a block.

The existing narrow powder room space presented a challenge because of the limited space. A custom sink was made to appropriate a small niche within the wall to maximize the use of the existing volume. Within the niche, the sink/countertop and ceiling are made of solid teak. The lightness and elemental nature of the stairway makes the simple rectangular volume of the perimeter enclosure, by way of contrast, the dominant form in the space.

Upstairs the built-in desk unit provides ample space for two people to work and also serves to divide the open space into two zones: the main bedroom area and a small corner alcove with a built-in upholstered seating area for reading and watching TV. Translucent glass at all the openings on this level allows light to penetrate the master bedroom and closet as well as the stairwell.

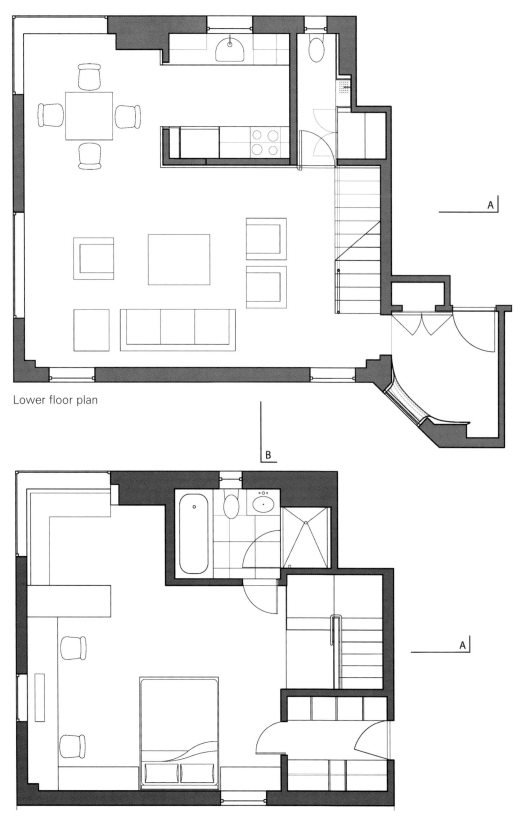

As seen in the floor plan, a sculpted, curved plaster wall in the entryway unifies what were previously three separate wall panels into a single gesture.

The first floor toilet and kitchen are contained within a seamless Sapele-faced box. The kitchen itself is carved out of this box and is clad in pale green Corian.

A|

Lower floor plan

B|

A|

Upper floor plan

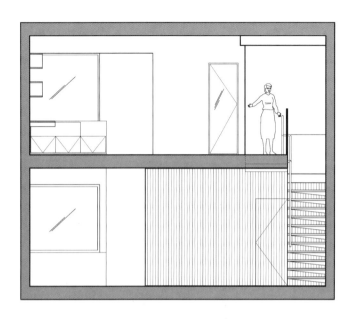

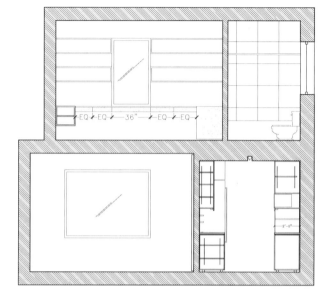

Section AA

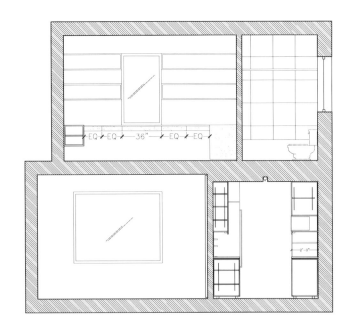

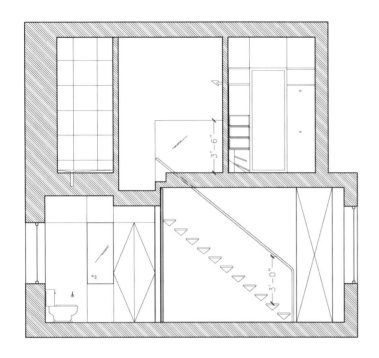

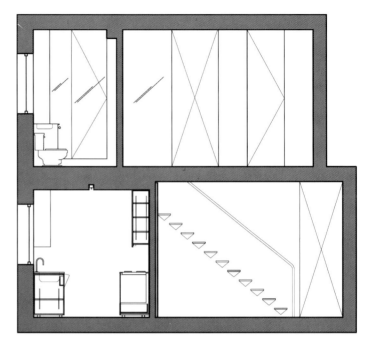

Section BB

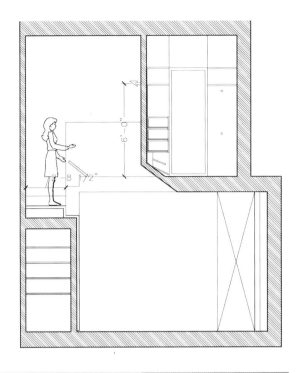

Eduard Samsó

Apartment Putxet

Photographs: Jordi Miralles

Barcelona , Spain

The 129.6 sq.m. apartment has been conceived as a single space, defined as such not only by the removal of partitions but by the choice of furniture and materials, that confer homogeneity and versatility upon the space. Floating parquet flooring, in oak, has been laid throughout the apartment, except in the bathroom, and the different areas have been separated by means of changing levels and low walls.

The dining room area is characterized by a series of pieces of furniture of a light appearance, that hardly disrupt the otherwise carefully homogenized atmosphere. Behind a low wall and on a lower level is the kitchen. Wood and steel lend this area a functional tone that is not devoid of a certain warmth.

The bedroom is at the other end of the apartment, on another level three steps down, next to the terrace. Separating this from the living room area is another low wall that offers some privacy and provides the living room space with a shelf. The bathroom is the only closed area in the apartment. The walls are dressed with travertine marble, except in the shower, where there is a floating deck of teak wood. Following the trend that rules in the rest of the house, the bathroom furniture is made of the same material as all the surrounding surfaces.

Natural light enters through the sliding doors from the terrace, flooding the interior. The avoidance of any unnecessary partition walls allows the natural light to shine through into the kitchen at the opposite end. At the same time, artificial lighting has been designed with the utmost care so as to underline the materials and enhance one's perception of generous space. Indirect lighting has been resorted to, with additional halogen lamps and spotlights around the perimeter.

The apartment is perceived as a single space, defined as much by the choice of materials as by the removal of partitions. Floating oak parquet flooring has been laid throughout the apartment and the different areas have been separated by means of changing levels and low walls.

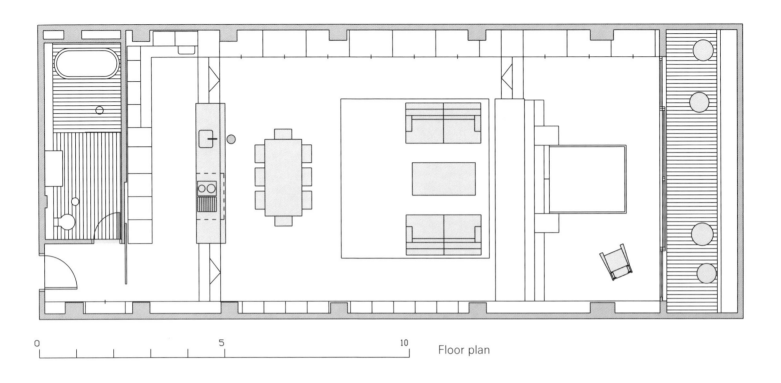

Floor plan

ARCHITECTEN LAB

Apartment V

Photographs: Phillipe Van Gelooven

Hasselt, Belgium

The client's brief called for a clear-cut, minimal living space that would provide a comfortable environment with sufficient attention paid to ambience. Because of his busy lifestyle and subsequent desire to relax at home after a hard day's work, the owner preferred an uncluttered design which would also have enough space to enjoy the company of friends and family when entertaining.

Since the structure of the apartment building already largely dictated the interior spaces, which had been conceived as an open plan, the majority of the work took place in the kitchen. The final design was a simple rectangular beam which, when not in use, looks like a row of cupboards. It is constructed in a dark stained oak, in consonance with the dining table and the wooden floors.

The library wall and the fire place are designed to exercise a subdued presence in the room and to keep a low profile. This was achieved by making them the same color as the walls and keeping a restraint on the proliferation of details. Thus, it is the objects and books upon the shelves that focus the attention.

The same principle was used in the bedroom and the bathroom, where subdued colors are predominant, and the same materials are used as in the living area. Glass mosaic in the same color as the walls creates a spacious atmosphere in the shower and bathroom area.

In the bedroom, the headboard of the bed was made of the same oak as the flooring, once again ensuring a tranquil appearance and drawing attention to the bed itself and the artwork on the wall.

On the whole the design of this apartment tries to project an image of the owner's lifestyle and background, so he can feel at ease and relaxed in his home, surrounded by his personal belongings and the memories collected over the years, in a setting which is reserved and subdued, placing most of the focus on the inhabitant rather than on the interior itself.

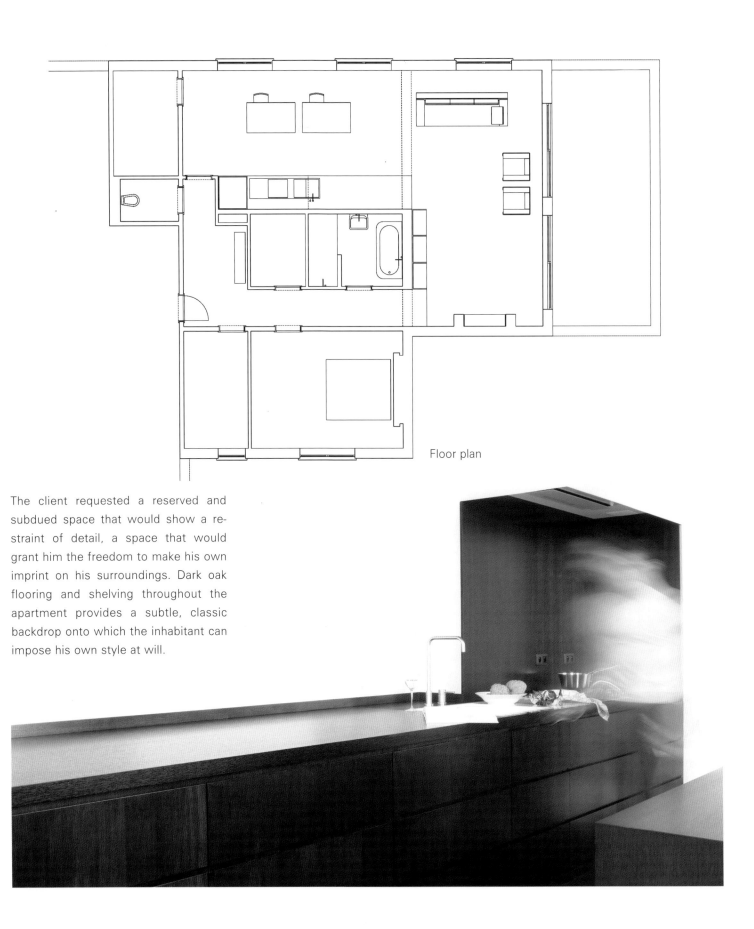

Floor plan

The client requested a reserved and subdued space that would show a restraint of detail, a space that would grant him the freedom to make his own imprint on his surroundings. Dark oak flooring and shelving throughout the apartment provides a subtle, classic backdrop onto which the inhabitant can impose his own style at will.

The same guiding principle of subdued colors is evident in the bedroom and bathroom. In the bathroom, a glass mosaic motif adds the necessary tone of lightness and visually opens the space.

Bromley Caldari

Emi's Apartment

Photographs: José Luis Hausmann

New York, USA

The fact that this apartment is a second residence has defined some characteristics of its design. The client was a Japanese business woman who needed a place of her own to inhabit during her periods of work in New York. The program required that the living room and the bedroom be considered as main priorities, as these were going to be the spaces most used. The windows of the living room are of generous dimensions and there is an unusually long sofa in this space, designed to hold the maximum number of guests. Opposite this there is a false panel which contains the complete musical and video equipment, with

Television and DVD. The bedroom is reached through a sliding door which also communicates with the bathroom and the dresser.

The sofa, which was designed to specifications, has a wooden frame and is upholstered in grey velvet. The pillows are of Thai silk and the table in the center combines the glass top with a base of tinted steel.

The shelves, made of ash wood, allow for a maximum rational use of space within the bedroom. So as to conceal them whenever it is considered convenient, the architects have designed the silk curtains that give the sleeping area a more intimate ambiance.

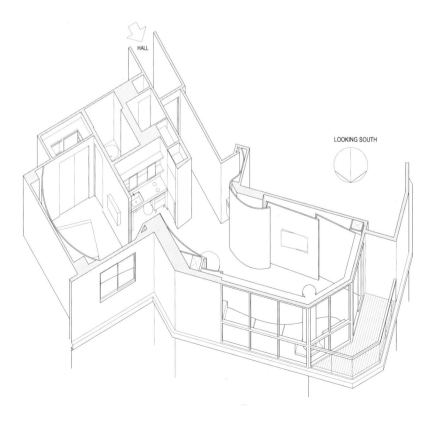

Curved wall panels have been inserted into what was once a predominantly rectilinear space, the end result being a much more fluid, organic ambience. The sofa, which was designed to specifications, has a wooden frame and is upholstered in grey velvet. The pillows are of Thai silk and the table in the center combines a glass top with tinted steel base.

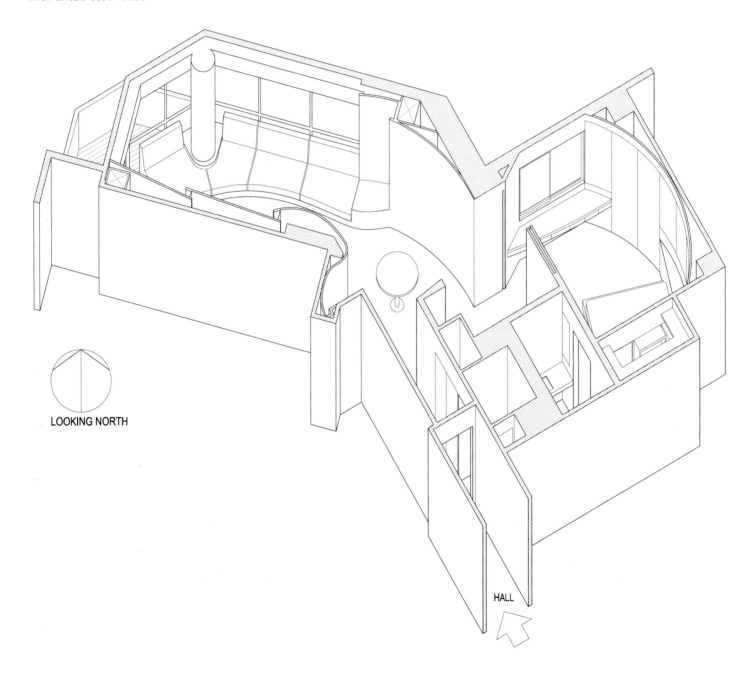

LOOKING NORTH

HALL

Floor plan

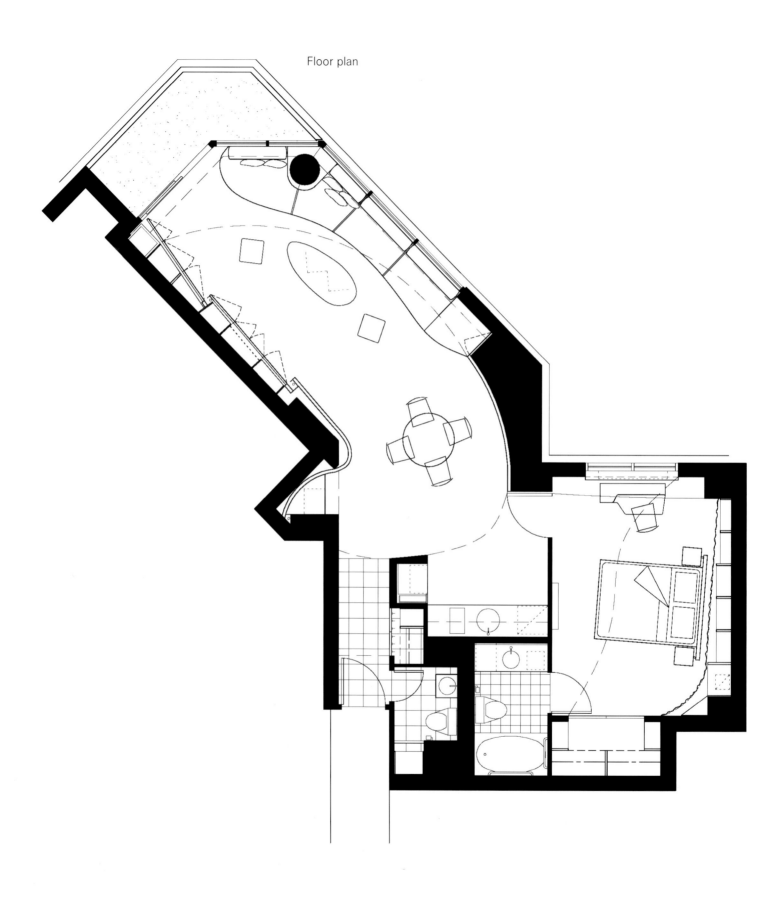

Rationality combined with luxury was the underlying theme for this residence which would be used only partially and, even then, for entertaining.

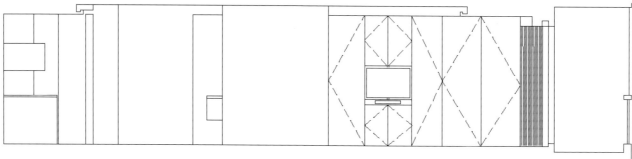

Living room, dining room, kitchen South elevation

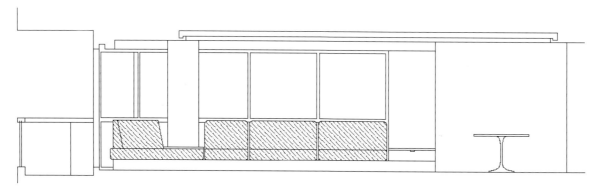

Living room, dining room, kitchen North elevation

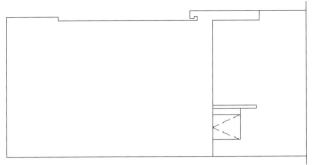

Entry / Tokonoma West elevation

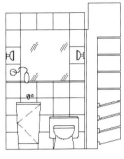

WC East elevation

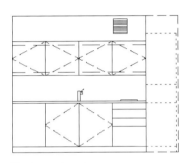

Kitchen elevation

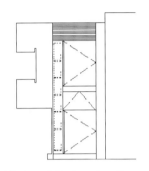

Kitchen / Pantry elevation

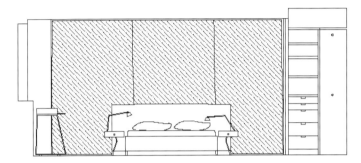

Bed room East elevation

GAP Architetti Associati

Apartment in via Cicerone

Photographs: Filippo Vinardi

Rome, Italy

The first step in the design process was an unusual brainstorming session, requested by the clients, a young couple with two children. After a tiring yet fun Sunday spent in front of a blackboard and a bottle of white wine, the key concepts for the design were defined: transparency, materialization, flexibility, etc.

The project called for the renovation of an apartment on the second floor of a courtyard building built in the last century in load-bearing masonry. The apartment was divided into two units, which were to be reconnected, with a total floor area of 1399 sq ft (130 sq m). The state of conservation was rather precarious: the paving was damaged and layered; the windows and doors were in a poor state; the wall finishing in some of the rooms was of low quality and full of cracks; the systems were all concentrated in one wet zone. Another interesting feature is the height of the interior spaces at an unusual 13.06 feet (3.98 m).

The clients wanted a large living room and kitchen, a series of work-study areas, the main bedroom, bedrooms for the two children, a space for a live-in nanny, the services, including a small bathroom for guests, and a laundry room.

Given the basic premises, the project found its inspiration in demolishing as much as possible of the existing: in other words, the removal of any non load-bearing elements (in this regard a floor slab dropped some centimeters after the removal of a light partition wall on which it rested, creating immediate problems with the building's residents). The resulting space became a functional block that defines the use of spaces that were otherwise undefined. This block thickens the central wall and generates a plan that is organized in strips: from the interior they include a hallway, the spine wall, the functional zone and, finally, the apartment proper.

All paving, with the exclusion of the service area, is in saw-cut slate in a running pattern of parallel strips, laid orthogonally with respect to the main organization of the strips in plan. The walls are finished in white stucco; a few walls have been clad in sliding, light diffusing backlit glass panels (the hallway); the main volume features a glass block wall that illuminates the wardrobes behind it.

The significant use of glass allows for a dematerialization of those walls that could not otherwise be eliminated, often in the corridor onto which the narrow entry faces. The metal pieces are painted in anthracite colored ferro-micaceous paint. The wood elements are in waxed, bleached maple.

Due to the previously unexpected fact that the entire building suffers from problems of settlement, which have caused the facade to rotate towards the exterior, with a tendency for detachment from the main building volume, it was necessary to carry out consolidation work using resins to fill the fissures beneath the stucco finish.

The existing shell was entirely stripped of all non load-bearing elements. The metal parts of the new organizational unit that was subsequently designed and installed are painted in anthracite colored ferro-micaceous paint. The wood elements, in contrast, are in bleached and waxed maple.

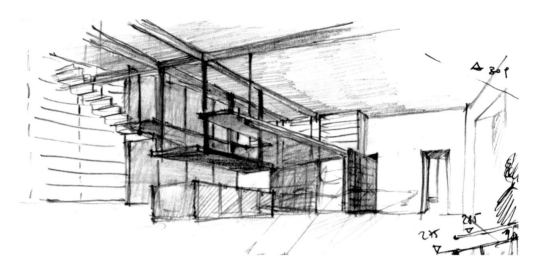

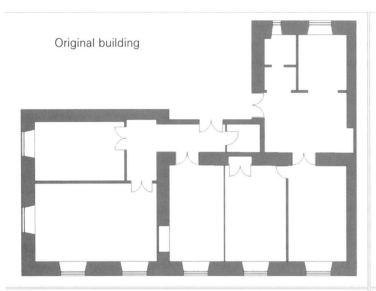

Original building

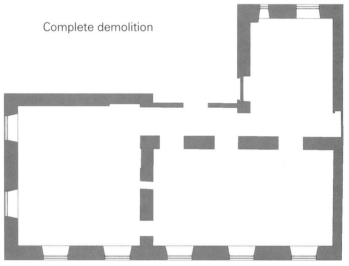

Complete demolition

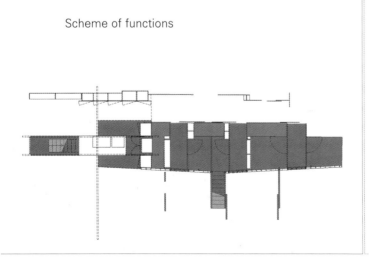

Scheme of functions

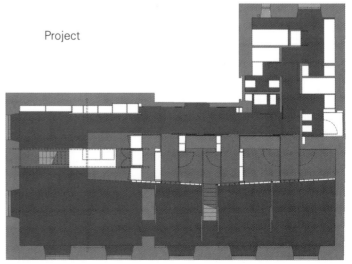

Project

Entrance floor plan

1. Entrance
2. Folding stair
3. Kitchen
4. Living room - dining room
5. Dressing room
6. Parent's bed
7. Children's room
8. Bathroom
9. Guest bathroom
10. Washer - service area

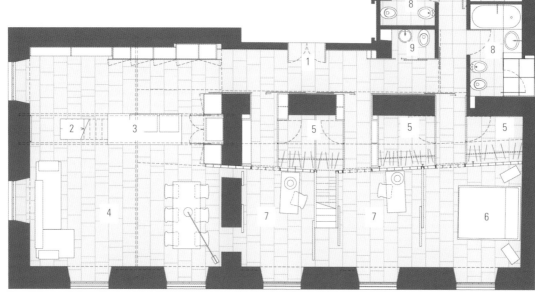

Upper floor plan
 1. Folding stair
 2. Studio
 3. Children's bed
 4. Children's closet
 5. Private study area

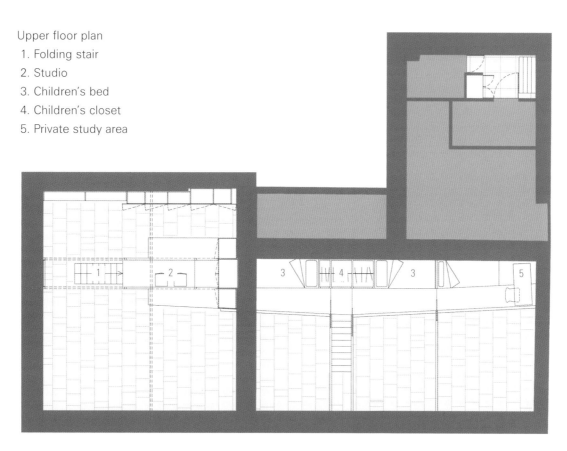

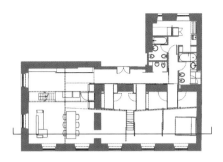

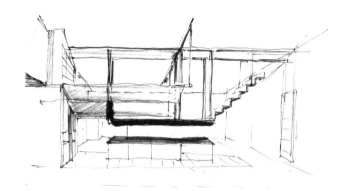

Longitudinal section
1. Folding stair
2. Kitchen
3. Studio
4. Children's room
5. Children's bed
6. Parent's bed
7. Private study area

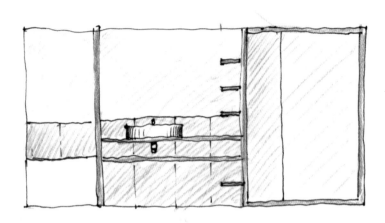

The unusually high ceilings (13 ft or nearly 4 m) enabled a great deal of freedom for inserting new structures and divisions. Almost all of the paving has been done in saw-cut slate set in a running pattern of parallel strips, laid orthogonally with respect to the main organization of the strips in plan.

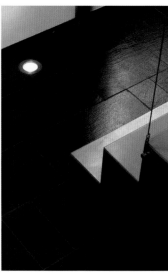

Ujo Pallarés. Ars Spatium

Apartment Maru

Photographs: Jordi Miralles

Barcelona, Spain

The commission consisted in the total renovation for a family of four, of an apartment situated in the 'part alta' (upper district) of Barcelona, on the hillside of Collcerola, with outstanding views of the city.

The apartment has a net floor surface of 140 sq. m. plus the terrace, distributed in 2 clearly differentiated areas. The area to the right of the main entrance is oriented south, opens onto the views of Barcelona from the terrace, and contains the kitchen, the dining room and the living area; the other is on the north side of the building and contains the two children's rooms, the bathroom and the master bedroom suite.

The seminal idea that generated the rest of the project was getting the kitchen and the dining and living areas to have as fluid a visual connection as possible, while retaining their separate characteristic independence, a feature that the clients insisted on. This unification was achieved by using sheets of transparent glass to close the gaps above the cabinetry that effected the separations between the hallway, the kitchen, the dining area and the sitting room.

The choice of materials used in the project obeys the functional distribution plan. Wenghé wood has been used for the flooring throughout the house, except inside the showers which have been custom-made out of black slate tiles, and for the cabinetwork that separates the various different areas. Glass, either clear or frosted has been used as a partitioning barrier; glossy enamel paint, quartzite and corian have been used for the finish of all the walls and ceilings, as for the work surfaces and wet areas in white, so as to achieve a unification of the general treatment. The few brush-strokes of color, mainly red - have been reserved for the scarce items of furniture.

Floor plan

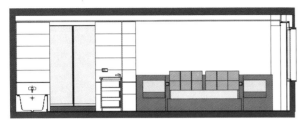
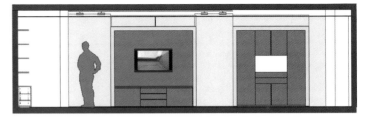

Longitudinal and cross sections

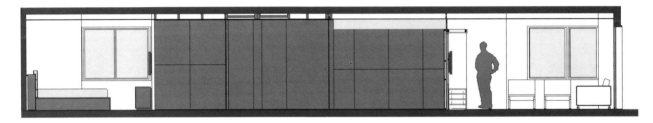

Filippo Bombace

Pink House

Photographs: Luigi Fileticci

Rome, Italy

A gay dance of luminous colored stripes underlines the indecisive geometry of a young couple's Roman home, situated in the heart of the so-called 'Città Giardino', a luxury housing estate built in the 30s in line with British 'Garden Cities', and further developed in later years. The apartment is part of a 1950's palatial villa, with a typically irregular geometry based upon the feeble but present positional rotations so frequent in well-to-do architecture of the period.

The solution adopted represents a careful balance between adherence to the budget and the firm decision to achieve a meaningful architectural result regardless of the constraints.

Consequently, risky floor-plan distributions which the apartment's extravagant geometry might have invited were abandoned immediately, and an extremely simplified solution was chosen that emphasized the long corridor (nearly 13 m) that characterizes the space. A glowing slit running along the ceiling further heightens the drama here and eloquently links the living area to the sleeping area at the other end of the apartment.

Immediate views from the entrance include a small cut-stone partition filtering the view of the day room and evoking the rhythm of a strip-code, and a system of sliding textile panels that outline the living-room area.

Placed so as to close off the living-room is the fully equipped, white enamel, steel-topped cooking island; storage 'columns' and the refrigerator stand behind, in white glossy enamel, glowing in the dark brown space. A cyclamen-colored custom-made volume conceals the extractor hood.

Opposite the kitchen is the dining area with back-lit sheets of glass, and a wengé-tinted oak table, designed and made to order, as was the upholstered bench. The equipment includes three swivel-chairs of perforated and lacquered steel and chrome.

In the hall is the sofa and the Liquid Crystal TV screen, which is fixed to the wall above the stone partition.

The ceiling's sunken neon lights, in colors ranging from purple to pink to orange to blue, are housed in grooves in the masonry. Built-in halogen spotlighting provides further options for emphasizing specific details.

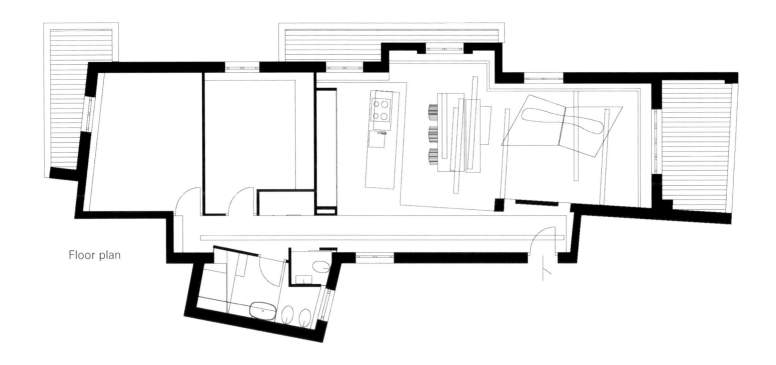

Floor plan

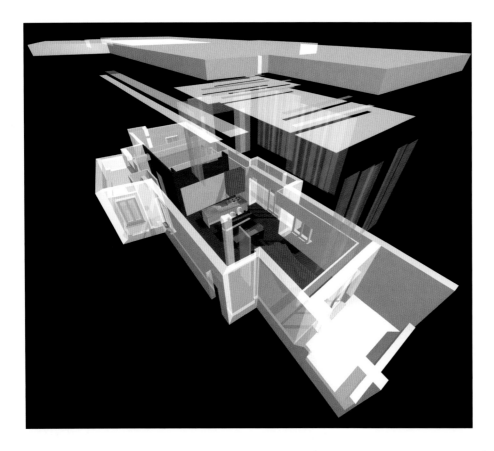

The dramatic 30-meter-long corridor culminates before a stone-faced partition, behind which is the children's room. The upholstered bench and wengé-tinted oak table in the dining room were custom designed, clearly following the lighting scheme of neon lights sunk into grooves in the ceiling's masonry.

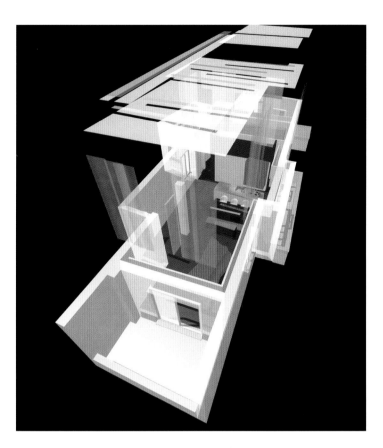
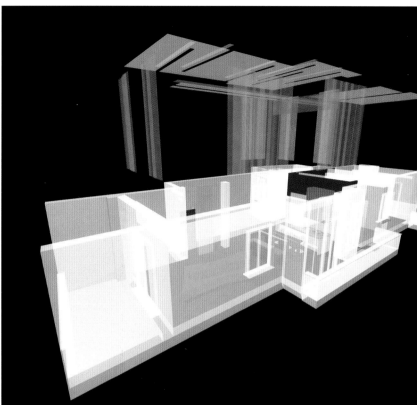

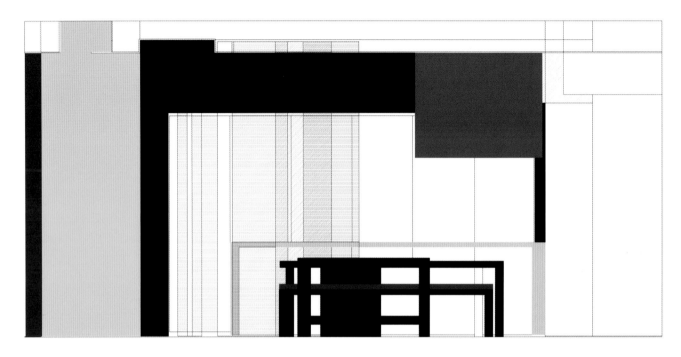

Cross section

In the master-bathroom a large masonry bathtub picks up the room's extravagant geometry while the remaining equipment maintains the luxuriously quiet color scheme, which is echoed in the color of the doors, and of the compact but comfortable laundry room.

Eline Strijkers

Unit 9

Photographs: Teo Krijgsman

Amsterdam, The Netherlands

The floor plan nearly always provides the basis for the organization of functions; when a dwelling is organized vertically, using a multistory elevation as the point of departure, the result can have a completely different character. In this particular dwelling-cum-workplace the functions are connected to the walls and not to the floors. This is how the existing shell of a harbor building (measuring some 2691 sq ft or 250 sq m) in Amsterdam-North has been approached. All supporting functions are enclosed volumes. Because work, storage, seating, eating, cooking, and sleeping are all components of a particular volume or surface, the space is almost entirely free of freestanding pieces of furniture.

The volumes unfold like independent sculptures, while at the same time making a free division of the space possible. Here, also, a vertical organization of the space is emphasized. There is a clear division between the ground floor and the other levels, which have been handled as a spatial whole.

The radical nature of the spatial concept lies mainly in the way that Strijkers has developed the unexpected materialization of her design, down to the smallest detail. At ground level, a different material was used to create transitions from one room to another.

The materials used upstairs give terms like 'domesticity' and ' coziness' an entirely new frame of reference. Despite all the attention paid to space, form, materials and details, the rooms are not ruined by a profusion of design. The prevailing casual atmosphere is the result of an unpolished use of materials, a sense of openness between the various parts of this home/workspace and, in particular, the tendency toward collective use.

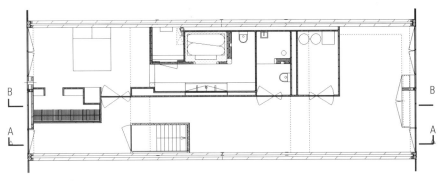

Ground floor plan

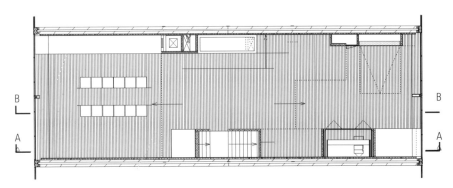

First floor plan

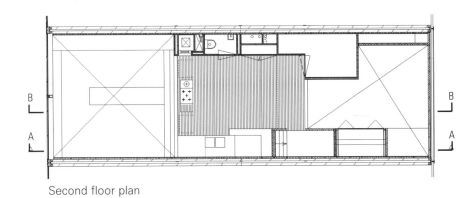

Second floor plan

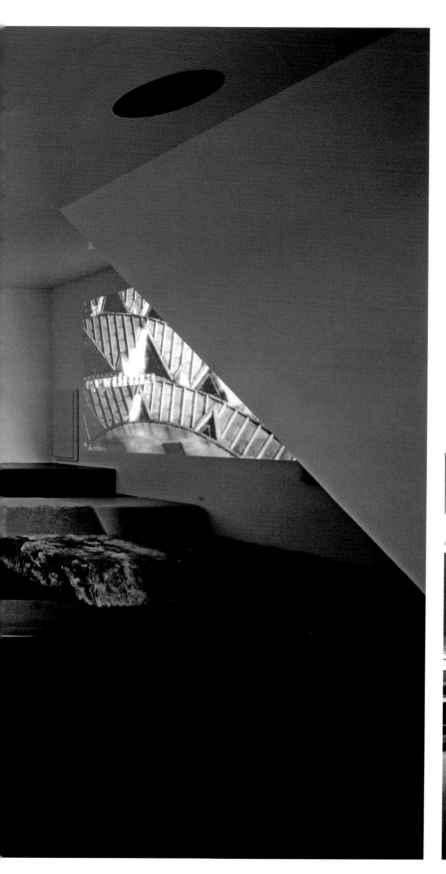

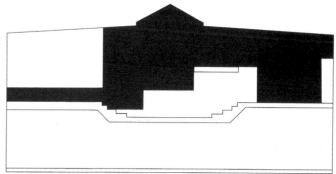

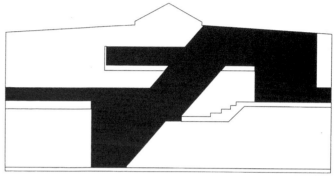

Concept drawing connected program

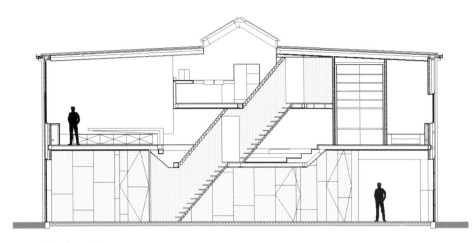

Section AA

The radical nature of this apartment's spatial concept lies in the way that the functions are directly connected to the walls rather than to the floor space. Because the work, storage, seating, eating, cooking and sleeping functions are all components of a particular volume or surface, the space is almost entirely devoid of freestanding furniture.

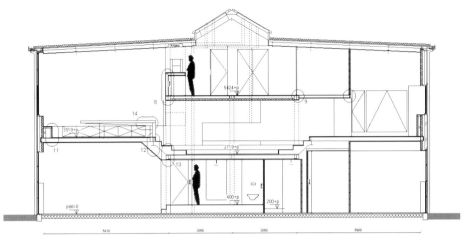

Section BB

Mónica Pla

Guillermo's Loft

Photographs: José Luis Hausmann

Barcelona, Spain

Before it was renovated, this old apartment located in Barcelona's Ciutat Vella quarter, featured a lot of rooms and little natural light. The deteriorated and neglected space has been transformed with the goal of creating a luminous and spacious residence in just one environment. The first step was to tear down various walls and to open up -structure permitting- a number of windows to permit the entrance of natural light. With no walls left to divide the space, the designer managed to provide the bedroom with intimacy and to establish a difference between the kitchen and the living area. To separate the bedroom from the main room and still maintain spatial continuity, designer Monica Pla placed the bathroom between the two. Accessible from the bedroom, the bathroom contains a shower which is contained in a box with partial walls. The sink, mounted on one of the exterior faces of the box, is completely integrated into the bedroom space. The toilet is situated next to the entrance door and a sliding door completely isolates it from the central living area.

To obtain harmony in the apartment, the furnishings were carefully selected. On one of the lateral walls, a piece of IKEA furniture unites the entire space, from the kitchen-dining room to the living room. As a result, the kitchen is integrated with the living room, creating a warmer environment. In the living room, Pla exposed a brick wall and managed to define the room's independence by means of a sofa upholstered in brown canvas from DOM. The dining room table is from Pilma. The lighting, also from Pilma, contributes to the warmth of the space, as does the wooden floor.

By studying the placement of the pieces of furniture and other objects that make up the home, the interior designer achieved a functional and modern renovation that floods a remarkable, diaphanous space with light.

Light colors, used for the furnishings, the hardwood floors, and the kitchen cabinets, present a uniform and spacious atmosphere towards the hallway.

To incorporate the shower into the center of the space required the use of a piece of furniture to divide the apartment's two main areas. A small stair leads up to the shower and the new installations are hidden underneath this platform, which reinforces our perception of it as a foreign element placed on top of the original floor.

The first step in the renovation was the tearing down of all dividing walls to eliminate the profusion of tiny rooms and the opening up of as many windows as the structure would allow. In the living room, the original balcony doors were retained and restored and the masonry of one wall was exposed.

A shower has been placed in a newly-created volume that separates the bedroom from the living room, while maintaining visual continuity. This volume is slightly raised, with the necessary technical installations set beneath

Cho Slade Architecture

Hochhauser Residence

Photographs: Jordi Miralles

New York, USA

The brief for the renovation of what is now a 2400-square-foot apartment (there were originally two apartments dating from the 1960s, each measuring 1200 sq ft or 111.48 sq m) was as precise as it was varied. The original apartments had to be unified into a single volume for a couple with two daughters, thus necessitating a complete reorganization of the space. The surface finishes (floors, walls and ceilings) were to be stripped and redone. The clients also wanted to maximize on storage space, and at the same time create as much openness as possible without compromising privacy. Finally, the views, particularly those to the south and west, were to be maximized.

These stipulations were met with the architects' solution of creating three zones. The "formal" zone is that housing the living/dining room, an open kitchen, entrance and guest room; the "family" zone encompasses the den, bedrooms and children's bathroom; and, finally, the "master suite" features a study, master bedroom, bathroom and balcony.

Each zone is arranged in a unique spatial configuration generated by the program and the location/orientation of the spaces within the building. The formal zone is a grand space occupying a full third of the whole house with new windows as wide as 14 feet (4.27 m) to capture the spectacular views and natural light of the southwest corner. The family zone is organized along a translucent colored acrylic wall that brings the spaces together with the soft glow of light. The master suite is a pinwheel of volumes arranged along the windows at the northwest corner of the apartment.

Maple flooring and cabinetry tie the zones together, while each space contains its own distinguishing elements. For example, cabinetry in an amalgam of black leather, stone and glass defines the formal zone, while a maple-colored translucent wall frames the family zone, and a dramatic plaster-sculpted Venetian wall/ceiling predominates in the master suite.

These apparently monolithic and monochromatic elements, such as cabinets and built-in furniture, are assembled from different materials with mitered joints to obtain subtle changes in materials at each surface. For example, the black built-in cabinets in the living room have black leather doors, black lacquered sides, black glass at the back and a black stone top. Because the mitered joints conceal the thickness of the materials, the material differences reveal themselves only when you are next to the object - from a distance they appear monolithic.

The "formal" zone of the apartment occupies a full third of the entire apartment and features windows as wide as 14 feet (4.27 meters). The living room is furnished in built-in cabinetry with leather doors, black-lacquered sides, black glass at the back and a black stone top. These apparently disparate materials form a unified whole, due to the mitered joints between surfaces.

Maple flooring is the unifying element between the spaces which otherwise feature very different ambiences.

Àlex Serra

Numància Apartment

Photographs: José Luis Hausmann

One of the requirements in the design of this four-story home was to bring a note of warmth to the cold feel of the original atmosphere, but without losing the masculine and modern touch that the client, a young bachelor, wished to transmit. To further this end a palette of gray and brown was chosen and the bare masonry walls of the loft were maintained.

The desire to bring natural light into the home determined the parameters of the design. Free and open access between the different levels guarantees natural illumination of all the rooms, with abundant light flooding through the large windows of the living room and the mezzanine.

The living room opens directly onto the terrace, which also serves as a dining area in the summertime. This space also features a small open-air swimming pool lined in blue glazed stoneware mosaic. The plastic and aluminum terrace furniture is from the Na Xamena series by Gandia Blasco. A large over-arching palm tree serves as the equivalent of a natural pergola.

Alex Serra has used tinted beech wood for the design of much of the interior furniture and fixtures, such as the dining room table, the bench, the low chest of drawers or the stairs leading to the bedroom. The center table is by Jean Nouvel.

The designer has used tinted beech wood for much of the interior furniture and fixtures, such as the dining room table, the bench, the low chest of drawers or the stairs leading to the bedroom. The center table is by Jean Nouvel.

Andrade Morettin

Prudência Apartment Renovation

Photographs: Nelson Kon

São Paulo, Brasil

The Prudência building is located in the central São Paulian neighborhood of Higienópolis, an area which, like the rest of the city, underwent rapid vertical expansion in the late 1940s, when this particular building was built.

The head of the project was the architect Rino Levi, whose work is fundamental for understanding the direction taken by modern Brazilian architecture in general and, to an even greater extent, in São Paulo specifically.

The chance to work on a building of which it can be said with no exaggeration that it is an example of some of the finest residential architecture in the city and one of the main works of a great master was an honor and a tremendous responsibility.

The organization of the apartment was quite clear: a wide distribution hallway articulated, with the section housing the bedrooms and living room, which is open toward the street, on one side, and, on the other, facing the courtyard, the services sector, comprising bathrooms, kitchen, etc.

The layout granted the occupant flexibility in coordinating the spaces, especially in the sector containing the bedrooms and sitting room. In contrast, the organization of the service spaces was intricate, abounding with subdivisions and small rooms, the reflection of a more hierarchical lifestyle which is no more.

The new program was based on two fundamental premises. First was the need to restore the elements designed for linking the collective spaces with the overall understanding of the building - such as the entry hall, balconies, carpentry and facades. At the same time, the program had to be clear and decisive in the interior and capable of reorganizing the spaces, with a new layout of the two aforementioned sectors - that which serves and that which is served.

A large installation was worked into the distribution space of the hallway, thus completely transforming the transition area between sectors. This part of the layout, once rigid and limiting, metamorphosed into a fluid and ever-changing space composed of movable panels that enable the integration of the surrounding rooms. Furthermore, this new organizational unit also serves as infrastructure, in the degree that it supports technical installations (electrical, lighting, hydraulics) and other functions, such as shelving, display space for artwork and storage for appliances.

The design and execution of this unit was meticulously wrought, each component having been specifically worked out and subsequently put together like a puzzle inside the apartment. The pieces are made from painted and bent steel and panes of tempered glass, in widths of 8, 10 and 15 mm.

The wardrobes and wooden partitions separating the bedrooms were redone, using laminated DM panels with Imbuia wood (a material which was also used on the doorframes) and sheets of cellular board. The flooring in the services sector and hallway was replaced with a white terrazzo.

While the original spatial organization of the apartment allowed for flexibility in the sector containing the bedrooms and sitting room, the former services sector featured an intricate layout of subdivisions and tightly hemmed-in spaces where the domestic employees once lived.

Floor plan

1. Entryway
2. Vestibule
3. Living room
4. Dining room
5. Hallway
6. TV room
7. Bedroom
8. Kitchen
9. Bathroom
10. Employee bedroom
11. Guest bedroom
12. Bathroom

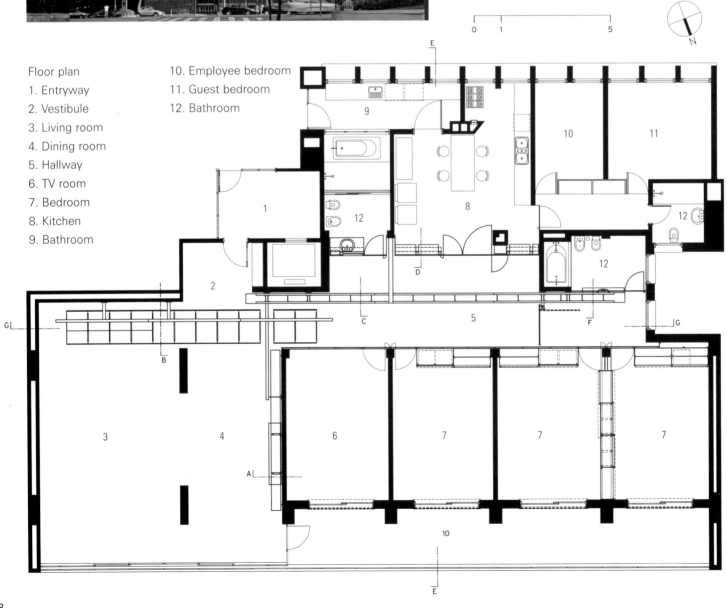

Construction detail

1. Clear tempered glass e= 15 mm
2. Folded sheet metal e= 4 mm. White electrostatic paint
3. Bar shear connector with nut and ¼" Fischer washer
4. Sheet metal e= 5 mm. White electrostatic paint
5. Folded sheet metal e= 5 mm. White electrostatic paint
6. Allen bolt in nickel-plated steel with nut and washer
7. Bolt with nut and lock nut with hexagonal head and washer

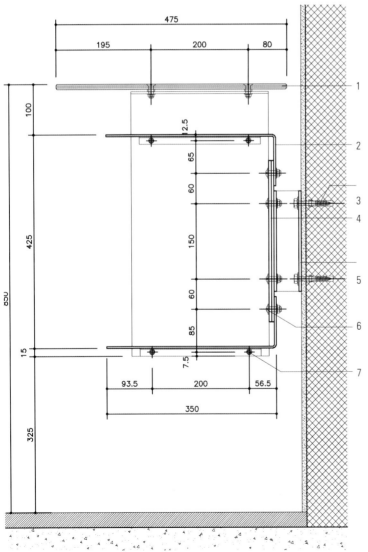

A large installation made from painted and bent steel and panes of tempered glass (in widths of 8, 10 and 15 mm) was carefully worked into the layout, creating a fluid space connecting what used to be two rigidly defined sectors.

The new installation now features movable partitions that serve to alternately open or close off the spaces on either side, while at the same time serving as shelving and support for the technical installations (electrical, lighting, hydraulics). The original flooring in the services sector and hallway was ripped out and replaced with white terrazzo.

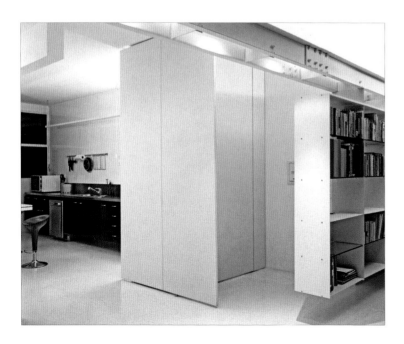

David Maturen

Apartment Zaragoza David

Photographs: Jordi Miralles

Zaragoza, Spain

Carried out in 2001, the project called for the complete overhaul of an attic loft in a building dating from 1903. The design scheme was centered on the search for the diaphanous and homogenous in the spaces, while ensuring that natural light reached every corner of the apartment. The furnishings and wall hangings were meticulously chosen by the architects, giving the space as a whole a note of elegance and warmth.

The flooring on the lower level has been done in stone tiles measuring 60x80 centimeters. In the loft, where the second bedroom is housed, the floor is wood. Plexiglass and acid-finished glass were used for the partitions and windows. The stainless steel finishes are perfectly integrated into the minimalist design of the apartment.

The distribution of the furnishings and fixtures defines the divisions between the living room/dining room and the bedroom and kitchen. The bathroom is the only space that has been completely closed off. The element that ultimately defines the spaces is the pronounced slope of the roof.

A metal spiral staircase set discreetly alongside the entrance, as if it were just another fixture, provides access to the main loft. There is another loft above the kitchen which is accessed via a folding ladder.

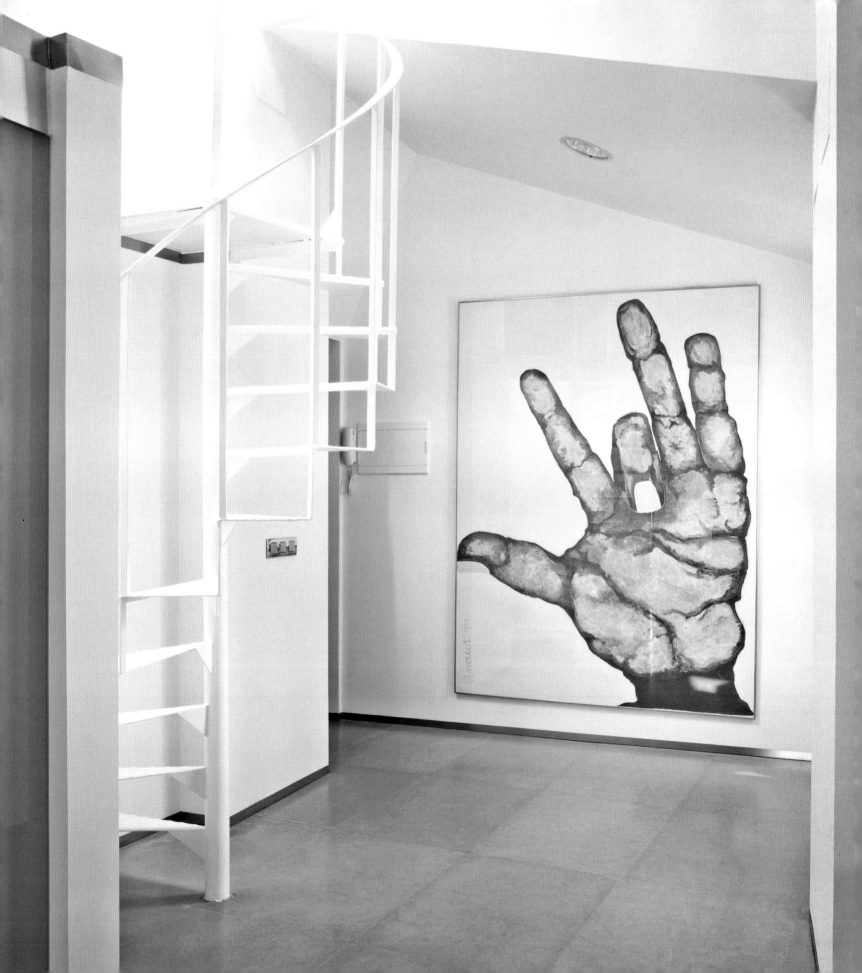

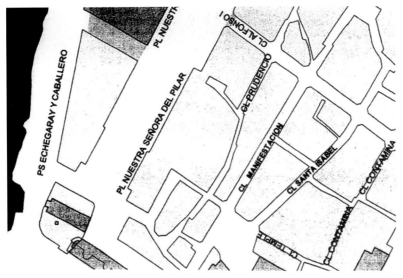

The flooring on the lower level has been done in stone tiles measuring 60x80 centimeters. Plexiglass and acid-finished glass were used for partitions and windows. The stainless steel finishes have been perfectly integrated into the minimalist design of the apartment.

Site plan

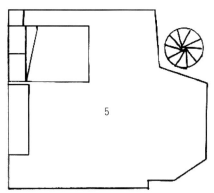

1. Hall
2. Bathroom
3. Kitchen
4. Living dining room
5. Bedroom
6. Closet

Upper floor plan

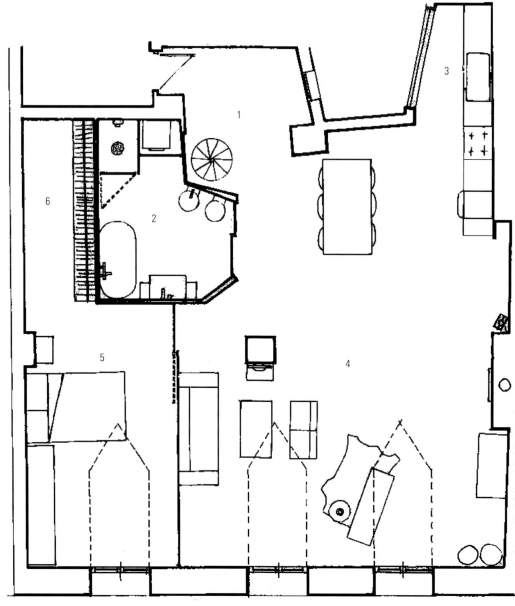

Lower floor plan

There are two separate lofts, each accessed via its own stair or ladder system. The secondary loft, set above the kitchen, features a folding ladder for easy access while a classic spiral staircase provides the elegant entry to the main loft.

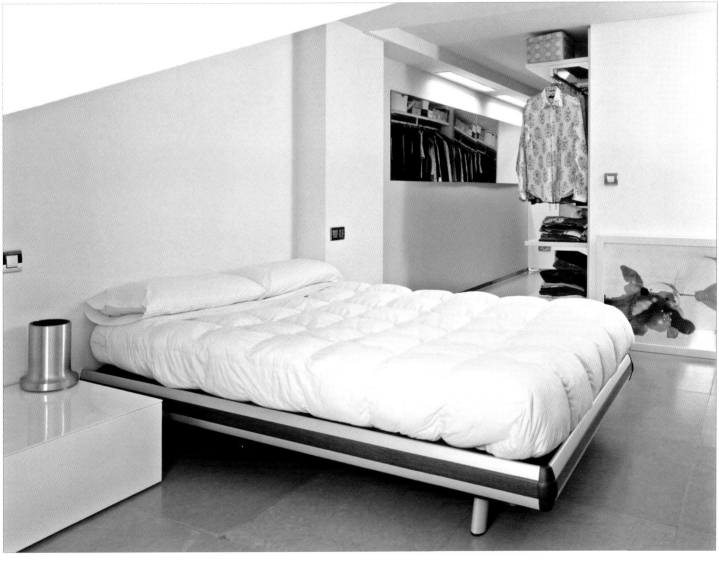

Drewes Architects

Cordes Apartment

Photographs: Christian Richters

Herzebrock-Clarholz, Germany

This complete remodeling of a conventionally laid out attic apartment grew from the client's wish for a loft-like living space. The removal of all possible dividing walls and partitions contributed to an open, continuous impression, but the centrally located staircase and bathroom present a barrier to a completely unitary visualization of the different areas. Yet at the same time, these basically disruptive elements are helpful as an organizing fulcrum around which the different functions of the loft can be grouped. As a result there is an open flow of space from the living area through the kitchen into the sleeping and bathing complex.

Eliminating the ceiling above the living and dining areas created generous vertical space and produced the option of the study gallery on the upper level which is accessible by means of a minimalist steel stairway. The kitchen is the core of the loft and is a hinge between the living and sleeping areas, with the countertop protruding into the living space in order to increase the spatial interconnections.

Visual connections and axes exist diagonally from the kitchen up to the bed and from the grand piano to the bathtub at the opposite end of the loft. The sleeping and bathing area is thus fully integrated into the open living space and is experienced as such by visitors entering the loft. For privacy, a massive sliding door of solid oak can separate the sleeping area.

A seamless floor of self-leveling epoxy, trowelled walls, steel, precast concrete and solid waxed oak reflect a simplicity and honesty reminiscent of the clients southern Italian heritage. The architecture takes a quiet and distant stand - a delicately differentiated background - liberating the space for the client's daily activities.

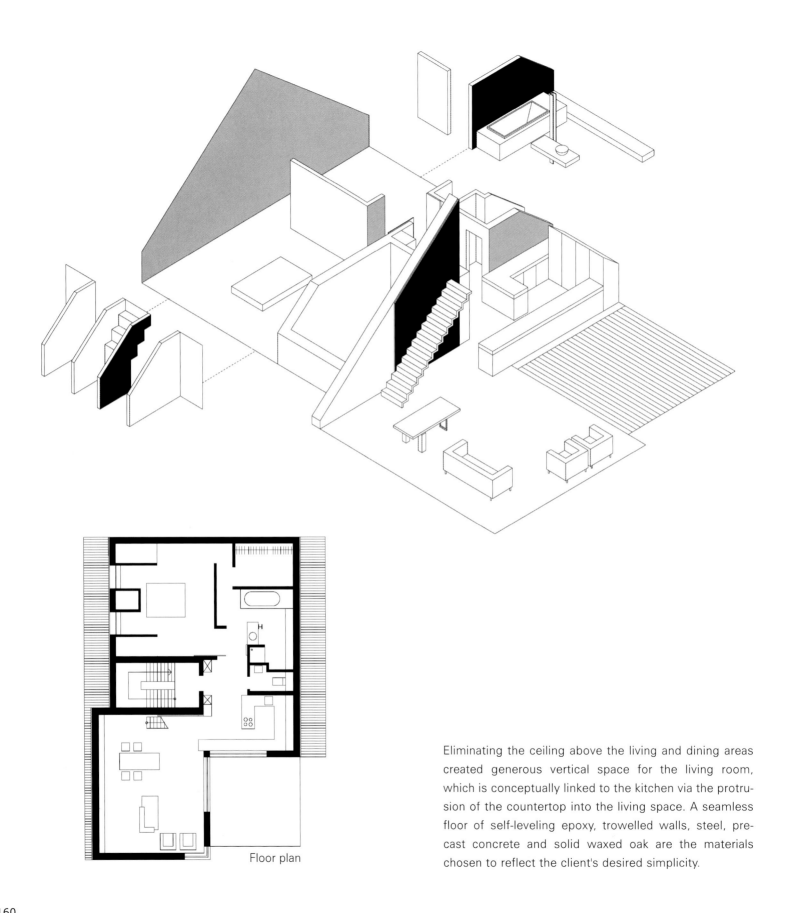

Floor plan

Eliminating the ceiling above the living and dining areas created generous vertical space for the living room, which is conceptually linked to the kitchen via the protrusion of the countertop into the living space. A seamless floor of self-leveling epoxy, trowelled walls, steel, precast concrete and solid waxed oak are the materials chosen to reflect the client's desired simplicity.

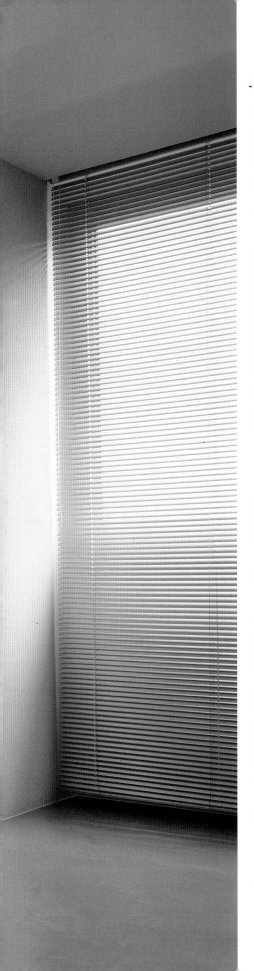